Historical Atlases of South Asia,
Central Asia, and the Middle East ™

A HISTORICAL ATLAS OF

YEMEN

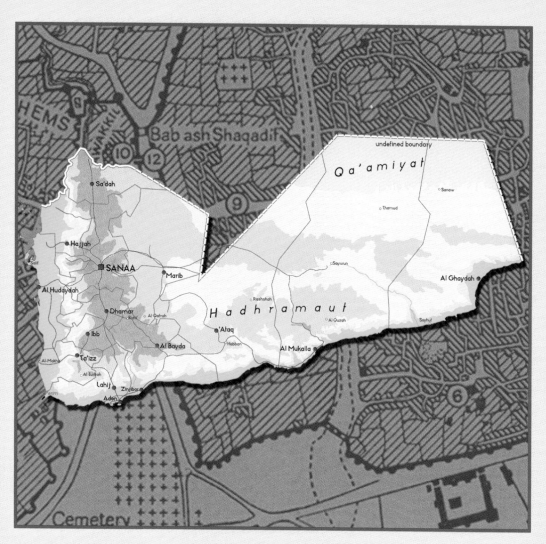

Amy Romano

The Rosen Publishing Group, Inc., New York

Published in 2004 by The Rosen Publishing Group, Inc.
29 East 21st Street, New York, NY 10010

First Edition

Library of Congress Cataloging-in-Publication Data

Romano, Amy.
A historical atlas of Yemen/by Amy Romano. — 1st ed.
    p. cm. — (Historical atlases of South Asia, Central Asia, and the Middle East)
Summary: Maps and text chronicle the history of Yemen, one of the oldest inhabited regions of the world yet one of the least-known Arab nations.
Includes bibliographical references (p.) and index.
ISBN 0-8239-4502-2
1. Yemen — History — Maps for children. 2. Yemen — Maps for children.
[1. Yemen — History. 2. Atlases.]
I. Title. II. Series.
G2249.51.S1R6 2004
911'.533 — dc22

2003055021

Manufactured in the United States of America

On the cover: The contemporary Republic of Yemen is pictured (center) along with its president, Ali Abdullah Saleh (top left), the Palace on the Rock located in Sanaa (bottom left), and an elderly Yemeni citizen from Thula. The background map is a detail of a 1946 map of Sanaa.

Contents

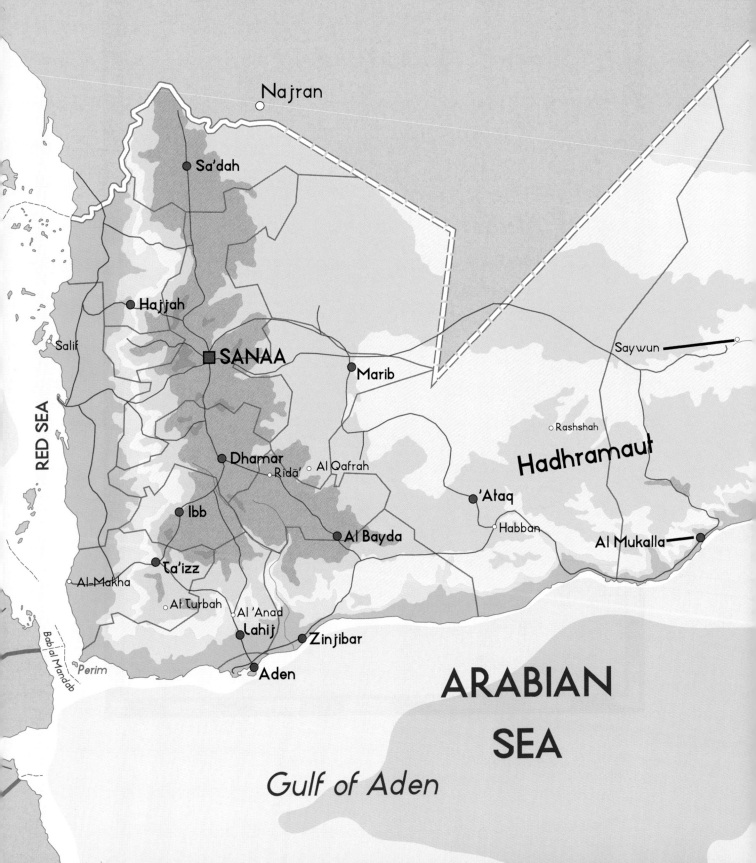

SAUDI ARABIA

○ Najran

● Sa'dah

● Hajjah

Salif

RED SEA

□ SANAA

● Marib

Saywun ○

● Dhamar
Ridā' ○ Al Qafrah

○ Rashshah

Hadhramaut

● Ibb

'Ataq ●
○ Habban

● Al Bayda

Al Mukalla ●

● Ta'izz

Al-Makha

○ At Turbah

○ Al 'Anad
● Lahij
● Zinjibar

Bab al Mandab

Perim

● Aden

ARABIAN
SEA

Gulf of Aden

undefined boundary

Qa'amiyat

○ Sanaw

Thamud

AL MAHRAH

Al Ghaydah

○ Sayhut

OMAN

INTRODUCTION

Although Yemen is among the least-known Arab nations, it is one of the world's most fascinating countries. Existing as a unified nation since 1990, the Republic of Yemen has an impressive history.

Located at the crossroads of ancient trade routes, Yemen is located in the southern Arabian Peninsula. It is one of the oldest inhabited regions of the world. In fact, archaeological evidence confirms human civilizations in this section of southern Arabia dating from between the first and second millennia BC. These discoveries indicate that the area, later known as Yemen, was important in the evolution of relationships between Southeast Asia and the Levant.

Yemen's strategic position at the southern end of the Red Sea was and is a key factor in its prosperity. The ancient trade of spices, silks, precious stones, and other valuable items is believed to have

This is a contemporary map of Yemen. Yemen is bordered by the Arabian Sea, the Gulf of Aden, and the Red Sea, as well as Oman and Saudi Arabia. Most Yemenis are Muslims, although there are small pockets of Christians, Jews, and Hindus. North and South Yemen unified in 1990 and became the Republic of Yemen. There had been great hostility between the North and South due to Marxist doctrines that the government of South Yemen had adopted. Floods of people fled to North Yemen in the 1970s. Yemen's first local elections took place in February 2001.

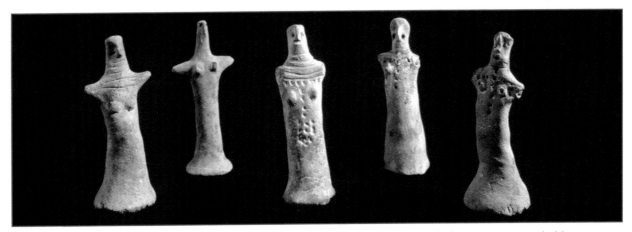

Above are small terra-cotta statuettes found in Marib, Yemen. Often the tombs of Chinese emperors held enormous armies of terra-cotta statues that were supposed to protect the emperor in his afterlife. The Etruscans were the first to use terra-cotta (literally meaning "cooked earth"). According to the Greek historian Herodotus, the Etruscans came from Lydia in Asia Minor. It is possible that they reached Italy by pure coincidence, after a famine had plagued Lydia. Other historians claimed that the Etruscans were natives of Italy and that their language was Indo-European.

either traveled through or originated in what later became Yemen.

Known initially as Arabia Felix (which means "Fortunate Arabia" in Latin) and in the pre-Islamic era as Sheba, Yemen is predominantly an Arab-Islamic country. Its Arabic name, *Al Yaman*, means "southward" and refers to its location in relation to the holy city of Mecca. At 203,830 square miles (527,917 square kilometers) in area, present-day Yemen is slightly smaller than the state of Texas.

Nearly all of Yemen's land borders are unofficial, which means that its boundaries are disputed by neighboring countries. In the north, it borders the area of the Saudi Arabian desert known as the Empty Quarter. Yemen's eastern border is shared with Oman. Its longest single border is a coastline that stretches along its southern and western sides. Yemen's southern shores follow the Gulf of Aden, an access waterway to the Arabian Sea and Indian Ocean. Its western shore runs along the strait of Bab el Mandeb (Gate of Lament) and the Red Sea.

As with most Arab nations, the single most important event in Yemen's cultural, political, and social history was the rise of Islam. Not long after the death of the prophet Muhammad in the seventh century, the majority of the Yemeni population had adopted Islam.

At one time a prosperous and fabled land, Yemen ultimately spent centuries in obscurity. Although the discovery of oil in the 1980s offered economic development for the nation, Yemen today still suffers from poverty and the legacy of its turbulent past.

1 ANCIENT CIVILIZATIONS

The area of southern Arabia that would later become Yemen is home to some of the world's oldest civilizations. One of the world's first cities, Sanaa, was located within its boundaries. Situated in the western mountains, Sanaa is now the capital of Yemen.

As early as the thirteenth or fourteenth century BC, southern Arabia was home to powerful kingdoms. Sheba, Qataban, Hadhramaut, Awsan, Himyar, and Ma'in all prospered on the fringes of Arabia's south-western desert. Although some kingdoms existed simultaneously, most flourished one after the other from 1200 BC to AD 525. As history unfolded, Sheba emerged as the most powerful of these kingdoms, with the Ma'in and the Himyarite kingdoms following it in importance.

Unlike many ancient civilizations, these early Yemeni kingdoms were not built on riverbanks but in valleys. The kingdoms were organized by farmers who later evolved into tradesmen and were renowned for their innovation. They constructed towering fortresses, inventive dams, and irrigation systems. These systems enabled the cultivation of agriculture in otherwise arid lands. This agriculture-based economy was eventually supplemented by money earned through trading. These civilizations capitalized on

These private residences are located in one of the oldest sections of Sanaa, a city that was once an ancient trading center. The stone and brick structures, some as tall as nine stories, are about 2,000 years old and feature windows created from white gypsum. Sections of Sanaa are now protected and restored under the guidelines set forth by the United Nations Educational, Scientific, and Cultural Organization (UNESCO).

their monopoly over the production of frankincense and myrrh, two of the most prized commodities of ancient Arabia.

As trade in these resins grew, so did this small region of the Arabian Peninsula. Adding to the kingdom's economic strength was their exclusive access to spices and the trade of other south Asian and African commodities, including ostrich feathers, gold, and ivory.

Although prosperous, the various kingdoms later known as Yemen and the

Frankincense and Myrrh

Frankincense and myrrh are gum resins found in trees in parts of northern Africa and Arabia. The resins contain oils that give off a strong fragrance when burned. In ancient times, frankincense was used in embalming and as incense. It remains the most important incense produced in Oman.

Myrrh consists of a mixture of resin, gum, and the essential oil myrrhol. Myrrh was highly valued in ancient times as an ingredient of perfume and incense and was also used as an ointment. At one time, the gum resin was also used as a stimulant. Myrrh is still produced in eastern Yemen and is sometimes used as an antiseptic.

Photographer David Forman took this image of a frankincense tree near Salalah, Oman. Frankincense resin is basically dried tree sap. People collect the sap in a way similar to that used to collect rubber-tree sap or pine-tree sap. The sap is then allowed to harden. Mixing frankincense with roots, spices, and seeds creates aromas with different nuances.

whole of Arabia did not find unity. The region was instead almost continually divided. At first, the divisions separated into warring kingdoms and then into rival Islamic imamates. These were territories ruled by an Islamic religious leader called an imam.

Ma'in and Sheba

The kingdom of Ma'in was ruled by a people known as the Minaeans. The Minaeans were members of an ancient southern Arabian kingdom that flourished between the fourth and the second century BC. Composed of peaceful traders, the Minaean community is believed to have been one of the more administratively advanced ancient kingdoms. The Ma'in civilization showed features of a democracy, such as elected leaders.

The city of Ma'in, the capital of the Minaean kingdom, was located in what is now the northwestern part of Yemen near modern Baraqish. This great dynasty was brought to an end late in the second century BC when Ma'in fell to the kingdom of Sheba.

Sheba was perhaps the most resourceful of southern Arabia's ancient kingdoms, existing for at least fourteen centuries. It is widely speculated that Bilqis, the biblical Queen of Sheba, traveled from this region to her meeting with King Solomon in Jerusalem in the tenth century BC.

Sheba was known as the Sabaean capital after its inhabitants, the Sabaeans. It was originally in Sirwah, now in Yemen's central highlands. The capital was eventually moved east to the city of Marib. This was an established stop along the incense trading route between the ancient port city of Qana (present-day Bir Ali, Yemen) and Gaza, Egypt. The strategic location, combined with efficient farming techniques and irrigation systems made possible by a large dam, made Marib the most prosperous city in Arabia.

The dam at Marib was built during the eighth century BC and stood for more than 1,000 years. Its recorded collapse in AD 570 flooded the entire region, a cataclysmic disaster believed to have been a significant factor in the fall of the Sabaean Empire. Archaeological discoveries in central Yemen suggest that the kingdom of Sheba experienced its greatest prosperity between 750 and 115 BC.

Lesser Powers

Although Minaean and Sabaean rule were preeminent in the northern and western regions of Arabia, smaller kingdoms existed in the south and east. These lesser powers—the Qataban, Awsan, and Hadhramaut—also existed along the

The Queen of Sheba

The Queen of Sheba is noted for founding the royal line of the kingdom of Sheba, perhaps the most powerful in southern Arabia. Known as Bilqis in the stories of Islam and Makeda in Ethiopian legends, the most popular story of Sheba recounts her journey to Jerusalem to visit King Solomon.

Believed to have been beautiful, intelligent, resourceful, and adventurous, Sheba was a diplomatic queen and an eloquent speaker. Although many stories exist about her quest, most agree that the queen traveled to Jerusalem seeking political and economic alliance because Israel's prosperity under Solomon was well-known.

Sheba controlled the southern end of the incense road, and King Solomon controlled the northern end. To ensure ongoing access to this important overland trade route, Sheba embarked on the long journey north. She arrived in Jerusalem with a camel train laden with spices, gold, and jewels to impress the king. Her mission was successful. The king was so charmed that Sheba became known as the queen of the Arabs.

Upon the queen's return to Sheba, she gave birth to Solomon's son, whom she named Ibn al-Hakim, which means "son of the wise man." Some Jewish and Islamic sources believe this child was Nebuchadnezzar; Ethiopians call him Menilek I, the first king of the Ethiopian Solomonid dynasty.

Edmund Dulac created this portrait *(top)* of the Queen of Sheba circa 1911. Because of its isolated location, Sheba's land was secure from military invasion for at least 500 years. Below are the remains of the five pillars of wisdom of Sheba's temple in Marib. Archaeologists are currently restoring the temple. As of 2000, it was estimated that it would take another decade before all of the remains at the site would be fully unearthed.

profitable incense road. Like Ma'in and Sheba, each also existed in or near one of the area's many *wadis*, making agriculture as important an economic factor as trade. (A wadi is a valley or streambed that is usually dry except when it overflows during the rainy season.)

For nine centuries, between the seventh century BC and the second century AD, these lesser kingdoms routinely fell in and out of Sabaean control. Unfortunately, they were never able to gain the power that the northern tribes enjoyed, and they eventually crumbled into history.

The Himyarites

The last empire of the pre-Islamic era emerged during the second century BC. Led by a man known as Himyar, the Himyarite kingdom ruled in southern Arabia from its capital in Dhafar from the first century BC through the first century AD. A small village in the Ibb Governorate in present-day Yemen, Dhafar was located in the northwest, north of Aden.

A direct sea route between India and Egypt was discovered at this time, which shifted the center of trade from the Gulf of Aden to the Red Sea. Second, Himyar theorized that by taking advantage of the monsoon winds, ships could sail this new route much farther and faster.

Because the Himyarites controlled the ports in the south and west, Himyar soon controlled the incense trade. By AD 50, the transition from caravan-based trade to sea-based trade was essentially complete. This transition was instrumental in the displacement of the Sabaeans by the Himyarites. Not long after this, southern Arabia came under Himyarite control. This ended the relatively peaceful

To the right is an alabaster stele that dates from the first century BC. A stele is an upright stone with an inscribed or sculpted surface often created to mark the graves of leaders or dignitaries.

To the left is a Roman bridge in Shahara, Yemen, that is 2,000 years old. The Shahara Bridge, which stands between two mountains, was built in the seventeenth century and can still be crossed on foot. As in the old days, women use the pass to carry grain and to feed domestic sheep. The view from the bridge is spectacular. On both sides of the bridge, the mountains part to reveal a glimpse of the enormous valley, where farms grow qat and coffee.

coexistence among the rival kingdoms in the area.

Conflict and Change

Himyarite rule was unstable. During the 600 years Himyarite leaders were in power, conflicts were common. The Romans, under General Aelius Gallus, attempted to conquer southern Arabia in advances that took place between 25 and 24 BC. Fortunately for the future of Yemen, the Romans were met with significant resistance at the walls of Marib, and they retreated.

In the AD 100s, Ethiopian armies arrived. Although they managed to occupy parts of the region for several decades, they were ultimately removed in AD 190 by the rejuvenated leadership of the old Sabaean dynasty. However, less than a century later, the Sabaeans were once again replaced, and the Himyarites returned to power.

2 THE RISE OF ISLAM

During the Himyarite period, there were a number of significant developments. Each played a dramatic role in the decline of the Himyarites and the other southern Arabian kingdoms.

The first of these events was the abandonment of the practice of polytheistic religions, or faiths that involve worshiping more than one god. At this point, monotheistic religions (those that have only one god), such as Christianity and Judaism, became widespread. During the fourth and fifth centuries AD, missionaries systematically converted many Arabian tribes from their traditional polytheistic practices to monotheistic Christianity, which spread throughout the area later known as Yemen.

Unfortunately for the Himyarites, with the rise of Christianity came the decline of the incense trade and the economy. This occurred partly because Christian churches associated the burning of incense with "pagan" rituals. As Christianity gained adherents, the importance of Arabia's two prized commodities, frankincense and myrrh, lessened. In AD 395, what had been a slow decline in the incense trade became a sudden halt. This suspension was due to the Roman emperor Theodosius, who declared Christianity to be the official state religion of the Roman Empire. With this announcement, the trading economy ceased, and

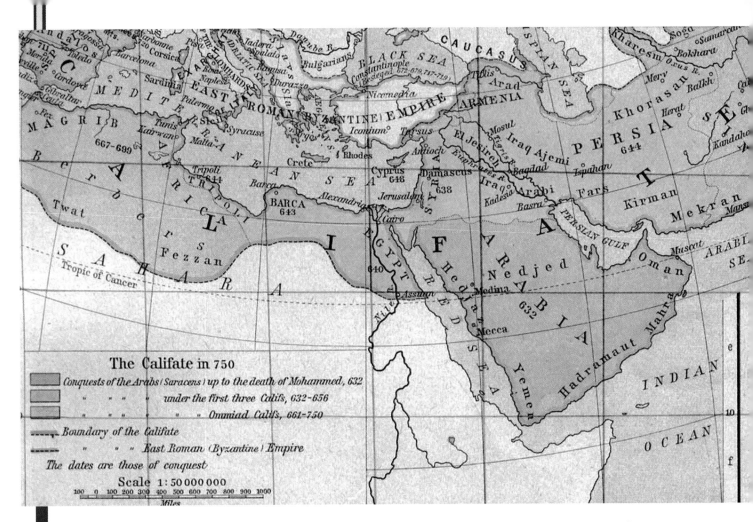

The Arabian Peninsula and the lands surrounding it are depicted on this twentieth-century historical map as they appeared in AD 750. The period between AD 661 and 750 marked the emergence of the first powerful Islamic empire, known as the Umayyad dynasty.

the foundation of southern Arabia was shaken.

Persian Rule

Both the social and economic environments in southern Arabia remained unstable for two centuries. With its base industry in disarray, the region was vulnerable. In 525, the king of Ethiopia advanced into southern Arabia, capitalizing on its instability. He seized control of the area. Some forty-five years later, the king died and the Himyarites turned to Persian armies for help. Together, Himyarite and Persian forces, then ruled by Sassanid leaders, defeated the Ethiopian Abyssinian army. However, the Yemeni kingdoms did not benefit when Sassanid forces took control of the region and incorporated it into their expanding empire.

Other events came to pass in 570 that would forever change the future of Yemen. The first was the collapse of the great dam at Marib. Because the incense trade had been so lucrative, the agricultural economy of southern Arabia had suffered for centuries. Local tribes let the kingdom's great dam fall into a state of constant disrepair for more than a century. When it collapsed completely, the released water destroyed many agricultural areas. As a result, the local population was forced to relocate, resettling throughout the peninsula.

The second event of 570 that would have a long-term impact on the evolution of Yemen was the birth of the prophet Muhammad. In sixty years, Islam would replace Christianity and change life on the peninsula forever.

The Islamic Era

Christianity had dominated the Arabian Peninsula for nearly 400 years. However, by the seventh century, a new religion known as Islam appeared. Islam was based on the teachings of a young Arab prophet named Muhammad. After his death, his revelations were recorded in the Islamic holy book known as the Koran. Badhan, the Persian governor of the area that would become Yemen, was a follower of Muhammad's.

Below is a historical map of the Persian Empire in 500 BC, which included the entire Arabian Peninsula. The Persians were interested in gaining the desert territory to protect the valuable trade routes through Arabia between the East and the Mediterranean. The coastal city of Aden played a significant role in this East-West relationship, as goods such as spices arrived to the sea port and then headed overland by camel to cities like Damascus and Mecca.

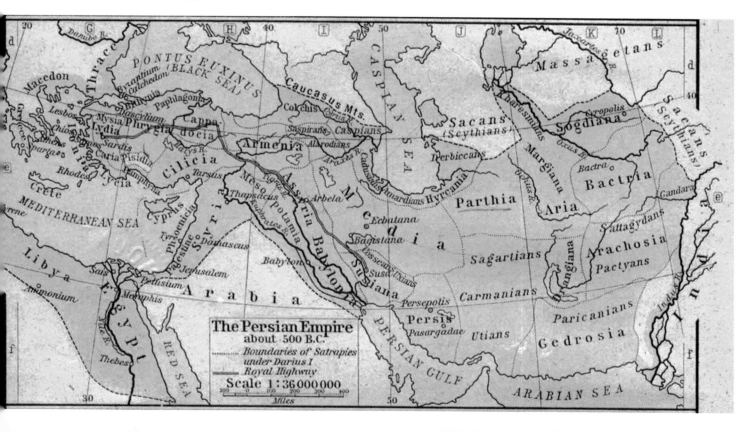

Islam

Islam is the name given to the religion preached by the prophet Muhammad beginning in AD 600. It is the world's second largest religion after Christianity. There are three historic sects, or divisions, of Islam, all built on the central concept of *tawhid*, or the oneness of God. Any person who follows the teachings of Islam is called a Muslim.

The majority of Muslims belong to the Sunni sect. Most conservative or fundamentalist Muslims are Sunnis. These Muslims follow a strict approach to religion, rejecting modern and popular interpretations of Islamic law. The next largest sect is Shia, whose members are called Shiites. The majority of Yemenis are Shia Muslims. Among the Shiites, the Imami are the largest group. The smallest grouping of Islamic followers is the Kharijites. These Muslims believe in a precise interpretation of the Koran.

Badhan converted to Islam, and the Yemeni people followed. Soon Islam gained adherents throughout Arabia.

By 632, the year Muhammad died, three Islamic mosques had already been built in Yemen at Sanaa, Al-Janad, and near the Wadi Zabid. Later that same year, the area was divided into three Islamic provinces known as Sanaa, Al-Janad, and Hadhramaut. Despite the population's near fanatical enrollment into the Muslim army (more than 20,000 of the original troops were from the area now known as Yemen), the country's position in the Islamic Empire was never strong.

Ruled by a series of orthodox Muslim caliphs, Yemen fell out of favor when the Umayyad caliphate came to power in 661. When Umayyad leaders moved the capital of the Islamic Empire from the city of Mecca in Arabia to Damascus in present-day Syria, the area now known as Yemen became a province on the edge of that empire.

The Abbasid caliphate seized control of the Islamic Empire in 750 and moved the capital to Baghdad, a city in present-day Iraq. In 812, Abbasid rulers incorporated Yemen into the caliphate as a province. At this point, small independent states and Islamic kingdoms began to emerge.

Islamic Cultures

Umayyad and Abbasid rule in Yemen ended in 819 with the rise of a local Islamic dynasty known as the Ziyadis. Founded by Muhammad ibn Ziyad, the Ziyad dynasty centered its power in the town of Zabid

This is a view across the old town of Sanaa. The minarets of the Great Mosque stand out against the sky. The Great Mosque of Sanaa is the oldest and largest mosque in the city. One of the oldest in the Muslim world, the Great Mosque was constructed in the lifetime of the Prophet and enlarged in AD 705. The layout is typical of early Islamic architecture; it has an open, square courtyard and is surrounded by roofed galleries.

in Yemen's southwestern plains. Zabid was near the famous mosque of Abu Musa bin Asha'ir, one of the first three Muslim mosques constructed in Yemen. Largely independent, the Ziyad dynasty existed for 200 years, falling further into decline with each successive ruler.

The Ziyad dynasty formally ended in 1012 when its last ruler died and left an infant successor. A period of power struggles followed, and two ruling houses emerged. The first of these was the Najahids, named for an Ethiopian slave who rose to power in Zabid. The second was the Sulayhids, followers of a devout Shia Muslim sect from the mountainous district of Haraz. Shia Muslims believe that Muslims should be ruled only by men directly descended from the Prophet. These groups would spend the next century fighting for control over southern Yemen.

In the midst of these battles, a woman became the head of the Sulayhid kingdom. Queen Arwa bint Ahmad succeeded her husband as ruler of an imamate. She ruled for sixty years and relocated the capital from Sanaa to Jibla, where the mosque of Queen Arwa still stands in her honor.

Meanwhile, in the north in the late 890s, another exclusive Yemeni dynasty was born at Sa'da. Yahya bin Hussein bin Qasim ar-Rassi, a direct descendant of the Prophet, was invited to mediate a war between two local tribes. At the resolution of this dispute, he

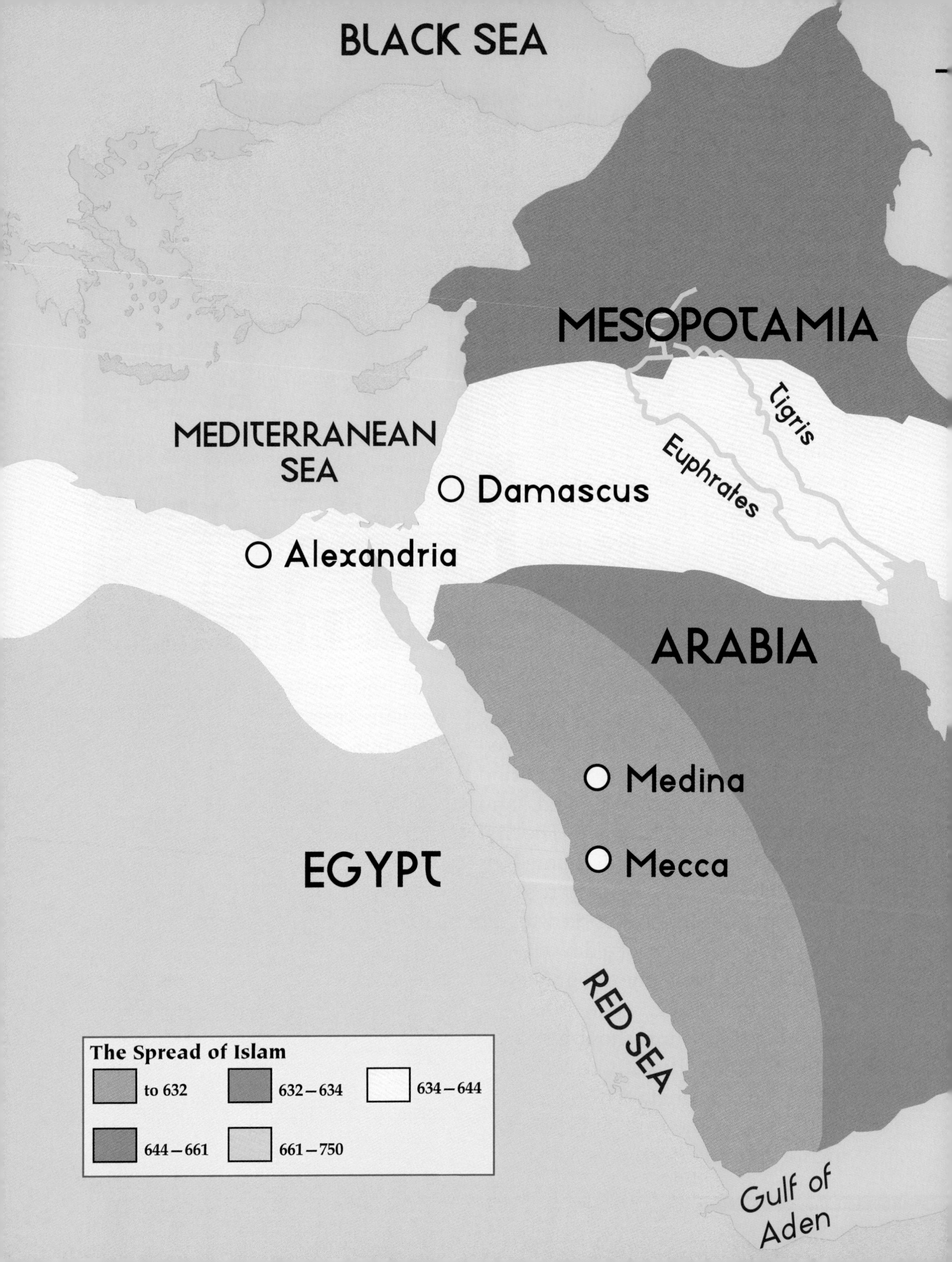

BLACK SEA

MESOPOTAMIA

Tigris

Euphrates

MEDITERRANEAN
SEA

O Damascus

O Alexandria

ARABIA

O Medina

O Mecca

EGYPT

RED SEA

The Spread of Islam

to 632	632–634	634–644
644–661	661–750	

Gulf of Aden

Caspian Sea

Bukhara

Samarqand
(Samarkand)

Nishapur

Balkh

Ghazna

Kandahar

SASSANID
EMPIRE

Persian Gulf

ARABIAN SEA

The rapid spread of the Islamic faith, as shown on this map of the Arabian Peninsula, sections of Africa, and central Asia, is due in part to the power of Arab armies. In less than two decades, Islam, a word meaning "submission," reached Syria (AD 635), Iraq (AD 637), Palestine (AD 640), Egypt (AD 642), and the entire Persian Empire (AD 650). Today, Islam is one of the world's most widely practiced faiths.

This eighth-century AD Umayyad illumination is from the frontispiece of a Koran, as taken from the Great Mosque in Sanaa. The Umayyads were the first Islamic dynasty (AD 661–750). Their reign witnessed the return to leadership roles of the pre-Islamic Arab elite and the rejuvenation of tribal loyalties. The Banu Ummaya constituted the higher stratum of the pre-Islamic Mecca elite. Having entered into an agreement with Muhammad in 630, they succeeded in preserving their economic influence and gradually reintegrated into the political power structure.

founded the Zaydi dynasty. Yahya also preached the philosophy of the Shiites. His teachings made a clear distinction between state and private affairs. He supported political activism and emphasized war. These principles resulted in an exceptionally enduring kingdom.

The longest-lasting ruling house in Yemeni history, the Zaydi dynasty, was at its largest and strongest between 1918 and 1962. During this time, the area under Zaydi control was known simply as Yemen. In 1962, a revolution in northern Yemen replaced imamic rule, bringing a thousand-year era to an end. This revolution gave rise to North Yemen, otherwise known as the Yemen Arab Republic (YAR).

3 UNDER FOREIGN CONTROL

As the mid-thirteenth century approached, Islam was firmly entrenched as a defining characteristic of Yemeni society. But even sharing religion could not bring unity to this region. Dynasties were short-lived, particularly in the south, and three successive families ruled southern Yemen between 1200 and 1500.

After a century of fighting, the Najahid and Sulayhid dynasties disappeared. But for a brief period of chaos, Egyptian Ayyubids ruled most of Yemen for fifty years, excluding the northern Zaydi kingdom. Because the Ayyubids found Yemen too isolated, in 1229 the area came under the rule of a Turk named Al-Mansur 'Umar ibn 'Ali ibn Rasul.

The Rasulid dynasty began in 1229 and established its capital in the southwestern city of Ta'izz. One of the last Yemeni houses to rule in Yemen, the Rasulids reigned for more than 200 years. At times, they controlled most of Yemen from the Hadhramaut region to Mecca.

In 1454, the house of At-Tahir from the southern city of Lahej briefly replaced the Rasulids. After less than eighty years, it was dismissed by the Kathiris dynasty from the Hadhramaut. The Kathiris also ousted the Rasulids and successfully stabilized the region. Though the Kathiris were still in power at

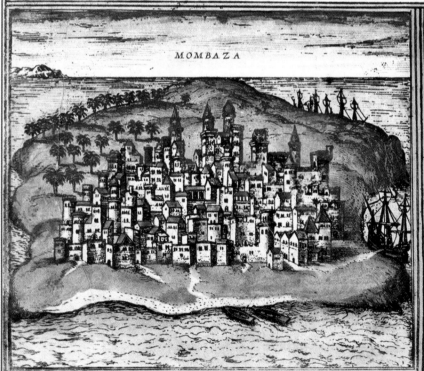

MOMBAZA

QVILOA

ADEN, Arabiæ foelicis emporium celeberrimi nominis, quo
ex India, Æthiopia, et Perside negotiatores conueniunt: vrbs
est magnifica, situ et structura bene munita, ædificiorum nito-
re atque frequentia celebris, muro et præcellis septa montibus,
in quorum summitaribus ardentes faces nauigantibus portum
ostendunt. Peninsulæ formam quondam obtinuit, nunc autem
hominum industria, vndique aquis ambitur

Cum Priuilegio

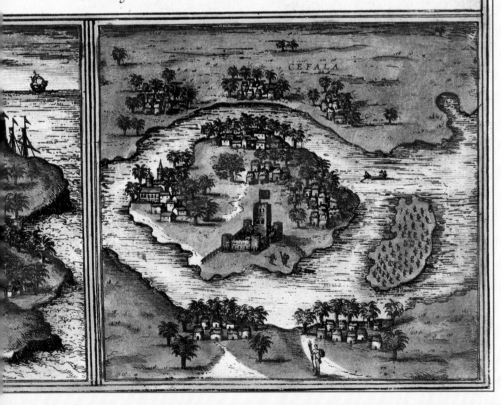

CEFALA

To the left is a picturesque collection of views of the ancient city of Aden. The natural port has been in use for centuries and has been recorded on maps dating back to the tenth century AD. Often described as Yemen's "gateway to the world," Aden's port and inner harbor now house and help maintain some of the world's largest container vessels at Ma'alla Terminal in order to ship cargo throughout central Asia.

The Islands of Yemen

The Republic of Yemen includes more than 100 islands scattered throughout the Red and Arabian Seas. Over centuries, many have been the quest of conquerors. The most notable of these conquests took place on Socotra and Perim.

The island of Socotra lies southeast of mainland Yemen in the Arabian Sea. For most of its early history, Socotra was an independent state. The Portuguese occupied the island in the 1550s, and the British took control of it in the late 1800s. When the People's Democratic Republic of Yemen (South Yemen) was established in 1967, Socotra was included.

Perim is a small volcanic island off the southwestern corner of Yemen, located at the entrance to the Red Sea. The French occupied Perim in the eighteenth century before Great Britain took control in 1799. It was also incorporated into South Yemen in 1967.

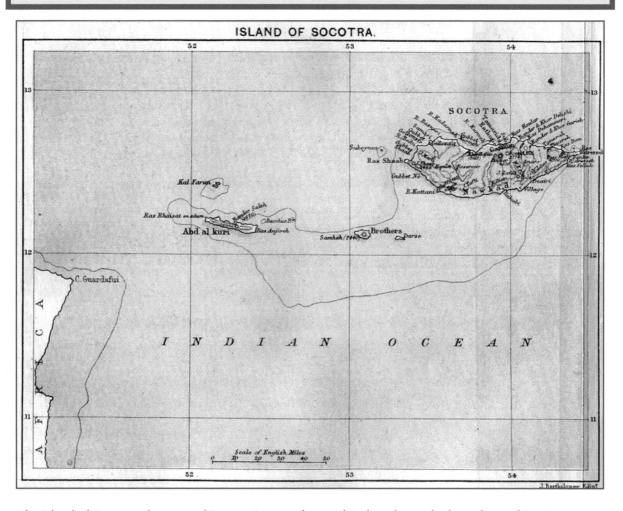

The island of Socotra, shown on this map, is part of an archipelago located where the Arabian Sea meets the Indian Ocean. Its name, which originated from Sanskrit, means "island of bliss." Because of centuries of isolation, Socotra is home to some unique species of flora, including the dragon blood tree.

the time of the 1967 rebellion and the creation of the People's Democratic Republic of Yemen (PDRY or South Yemen), they were significantly weakened.

The Ottomans

From the early 1500s, the Kathiris and Zaydi dynasties of Yemen saw a new threat in the region. The emerging powers of Europe were becoming increasingly interested in southern Arabia and controlling the east-west trade with India. The Portuguese were the first Europeans to arrive on the peninsula.

By 1507, the Portuguese annexed the island of Socotra in the Arabian Sea. Four years later, Afonso de Albuquerque attempted to extend the Portuguese presence in Arabia but failed. His intention was to capture Yemen's southern port of Aden. This unsuccessful attack encouraged other armies to increase their actions in the Red Sea. For the next seven

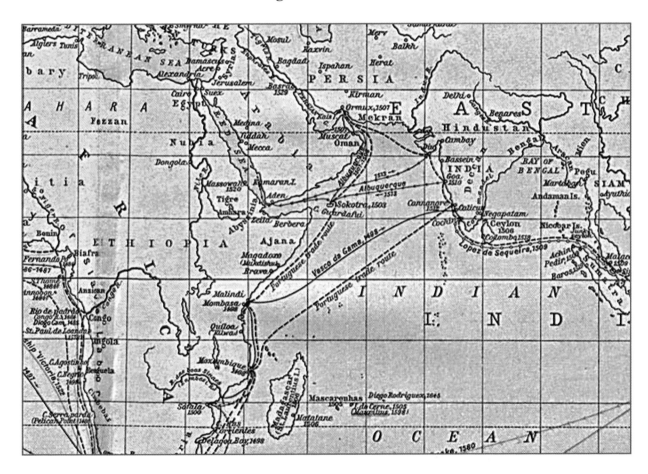

This historical map details the routes taken by the fifteenth-century Portuguese explorers Vasco da Gama and Afonso de Albuquerque. After da Gama located the direct sea route to India from Portugal in 1498, both navigators helped the Portuguese monopolize trade between the West and South Asia. In doing so, Albuquerque captured the islands of Socotra and Ormuz in 1507 in the hopes of controlling trade in the Red Sea.

years, Yemeni armies fought off advances by a succession of Ottoman and Mamluk Turks. However, by 1517, the Muslim Ottoman Empire, centered in what is now Turkey, had conquered most of Yemen. Ottoman forces were firmly in control of the Yemeni cities of

Coffee

The history of coffee is masked in chance occurrences. Though it is not exactly known where or when in history coffee first appeared, it is widely accepted that it was cultivated in Arabia around AD 675.

A number of legends survive about the evolution of the coffee bean. One such story suggests that a sheepherder discovered the stimulating effect of coffee by studying the reactions of his sheep after they ate what he called the red "cherries" and leaves of the plant. Curious, the sheepherder tried the cherries himself and was scolded by local monks for eating the devil's fruit. However, monks soon discovered that eating the fruit helped them stay awake for prayers.

Another legend recounts that it was the coffee bean that saved the lives of a young Arabian and his followers who were banished to the desert. Faced with starvation, the Arab directed his companions to boil the cherries and drink the liquid. The men's survival, after drinking the liquid, was taken as a religious sign by the residents of Mocha (Al-Makha). Both the plant and its beverage were named mocha to honor the miraculous event.

By the sixteenth century, extensive planting of coffee occurred in Arabia. As the worldwide consumption increased, Dutch and British trading companies soon successfully cultivated coffee plants and processed coffee beans. In the early 1700s, coffee plants were smuggled out of the area later known as Yemen and replanted in Indonesia and Latin America. In less than two decades, the Arabian coffee business was all but destroyed due to the less expensive crops being produced by descendant plants of Yemen's *Coffea arabica*.

Diego Lezama Orezzoli took this photo of Arabian coffee cherries on a tree in Mococa, Brazil. Coffee cherries were transported from Ethiopia to the Arabian Peninsula and were grown in what today is the country of Yemen. From there, coffee traveled to Turkey, where coffee beans were roasted for the first time over open fires. The roasted beans were crushed, boiled in water, and cooled. People then drank the liquid. This created a crude version of the coffee we enjoy today.

Ta'izz, Aden, and Sanaa by 1548. The first period of Ottoman rule in Yemen was under way.

Over the next century, many positive economic developments occurred in Yemen. One of the most significant was the tremendous growth of Yemen's coffee trading business, which started in the fifteenth century. The city of Mocha (Al-Makha) on the southernmost shore of the Red Sea evolved into the world's most important coffee port. By the early 1600s, British and Dutch trading companies had opened profitable factories in Mocha.

Resurgence of Yemeni Control

While Ottoman control in southern Yemen remained stable, the northern Zaydi state wanted to bring freedom to all Yemeni citizens who were oppressed by Ottoman Turks. In 1636, it achieved that goal.

With the Turks removed, the prospects for an independent Yemen seemed possible. In fact,

life in Yemen in the late 1600s and early 1700s was glorious. The Zaydi state was growing, eventually extending from the Hadhramaut to Asir (in present-day Saudi Arabia) in the north. The economy, boosted by the coffee trade, was blossoming.

Unfortunately, coffee plants were smuggled out of Yemen and replanted in Brazil and Indonesia. Within a span of twenty years, the demand for Yemeni coffee had vanished. By 1740, the Zaydi economy crumbled. The Zaydis were also facing the challenges of internal strife and external threats to their authority.

This eighteenth-century historical map, housed in the Library of Congress, is a detail showing the southern tip of the Arabian Peninsula. At the time of the map's creation in 1721, Yemen enjoyed relative stability compared to the later attacks its citizens endured from invading Arab armies and the occupation of British forces in 1839.

Outsider Arabian armies known as Wahhabis mounted continual attacks on Yemen's western Tihama region, eventually destroying the area from the north to the southern town of Al-Hudaydah. Internally, local tribes demanded their independence. To this end, the sultan of Lahej took steps to block Zaydi access to the port of Aden and the Yemeni coastline that followed the Arabian Sea.

This single act sparked two dramatic events. First, it opened the door for nineteenth-century British occupation. Second, it began the process that led to the twentieth-century formation of two independent Yemeni states.

British Occupation

In 1839, operating from the island of Perim in the Bab el Mandeb, the British conquered Aden. By 1854, they increased their occupation to include the Kuria Muria Islands. Three years later, a treaty was signed between Britain and the sultan of Lahej. Efforts to further consolidate southern Yemen continued. By 1914, several Yemeni sheikhdoms joined the sultan of Lahej in the "friendship treaty" with Britain. The result was the formation of South Arabia.

Although the British presence in Yemen remained strong until the 1950s, it was not all-encompassing. The Ottoman Turks returned to Yemen in 1849 and occupied the Tihama. Twenty years later, after the 1869 opening of the Suez Canal, the Turkish position within Yemen strengthened. In succession, the Turks gained and occupied Ta'izz (1871), Sanaa (1872), and, eventually, Sa'da and the Zaydi capital (1882).

As the Turks and British expanded their control over Yemen, they eventually drew a line between the two territories. Agreed upon in 1905 and known as the violet line, this border remained intact throughout much of the twentieth century. It denoted the boundary between the separate North and South Yemeni states.

Unlike the earlier occupation, the second Ottoman occupation involved the territory of Yemen not under British rule. Turkish power was opposed during a number of uprisings led by the Zaydis and northern Tihama tribes. By the early 1900s, these uprisings strengthened Yemeni identity. The 1911 Treaty of Da'an gave Zaydi leader Imam Yahya ibn Muhammad authority over Yemen's highlands region.

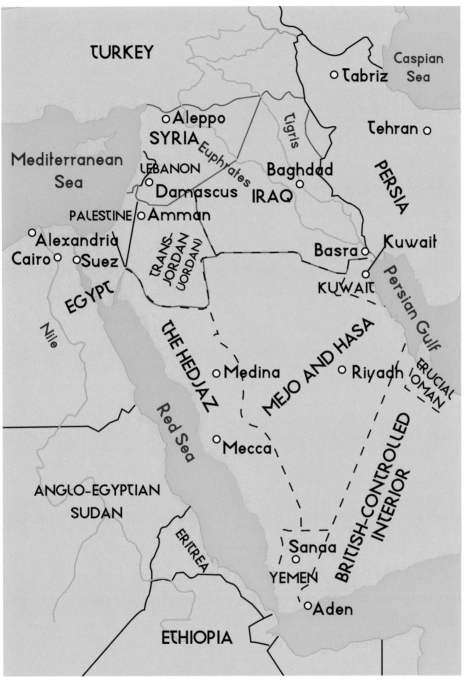

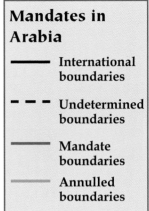

This map of Arabia illustrates how the Lausanne Treaty affected countries in the Middle East. The agreement, which was signed between Great Britain, France, Italy, Japan, Greece, Romania, and Turkey on July 24, 1923, brought a formal end to World War I and the power of the Turkish Ottoman Empire. Although North Yemen was considered independent at this time, South Yemen remained a part of the British-controlled interior of the Arabian Peninsula.

Less than a decade later, after Turkey's defeat in World War I (1914–1918), Ottoman forces withdrew from North Yemen. The Treaty of Lausanne (1923) formally ended Turkish rule. North Yemen was recognized as an independent state. South Yemen was still in the hands of the British.

4 NORTH YEMEN

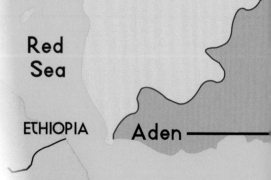

YEMEN ARAB REPUBLIC (North Yemen)

Sanaa ○

Red Sea

ETHIOPIA

Aden

Independence from the Ottoman Empire did not bring relief from conflict for North Yemen. Imam Yahya was faced with the obstacles of consolidating authority and securing borders. His greatest challengers were the local tribes in western Yemen and Saudi Arabian forces in the north.

Initial Challenges

As Imam Yahya acted to bring unity to an independent Yemen, his first great challenge came from the Idrisi leadership in Tihama. The northern Idrisi forces had previously allied with Yahya to secure freedom from the Turks. However, they continued to occupy much of the Tihama and claimed independence of their own. It wasn't until 1925 that Yahya advanced from his capital in Sanaa into Tihama and seized the coastal city of Al Hudaydah. He

The territory of independent North Yemen and British-controlled South Yemen are depicted on this map. The British control of South Yemen was later viewed as an attempt by the British Empire to control trade in the region of the Red Sea and surrounding Arab territory. The leader of North Yemen, Imam Yahya, wanted to unite the two territories but was challenged by the near constant infighting among Yemeni tribes. The Palace on the Rock (*inset*) is located in Sanaa, the present-day capital of a united Yemen.

SAUDI ARABIA

People's Democratic Republic of Yemen
(SouthYemen)

Gulf of Aden

removed the Idrisi leadership and gained control of the region.

Once in charge, Yahya advanced his troops north. As he passed Midi, a northwestern village in Yemen near the present-day Saudi border, the Saudi government became concerned. Until this point, the Saudis had planned to annex Tihama for Saudi Arabia. Imam Yahya had similar plans regarding the Asir region in what is now Saudi Arabia. The conflict became so unsettling for both sides that in 1934 it resulted in a war.

The Saudi Dispute

The Saudi-Yemeni War of 1934 was the first major incident in what would become decades of border disputes between Yemen and Saudi Arabia. Saudi forces reached Al Hudaydah very quickly, and Yahya was forced to accept peace on Saudi terms.

Under the terms of the Taif Treaty, peace for Yemen meant the annexation of two northern territories. According to the treaty, the northern Yemeni regions of Asir and Najran were placed under forty years of "temporary" Saudi rule. However, in 1947, the Saudis extended their rule over these areas for another two decades. In 1994, when the time came to renegotiate and return Asir and Najran

to Yemen, Saudi Arabia declined. Instead, it claimed permanent ownership of the two territories. It also demanded that Western oil companies exploring the "disputed territories" leave immediately and revoked Yemeni work visas. The result was another round of border clashes between Saudis and Yemenis.

As neither country wanted war, both sides worked to reach an agreement. By February 1995, Yemeni relations with Saudi Arabia began to normalize with the signing of a Memorandum of Understanding. The memorandum established guidelines for the reinstatement of Yemeni work visas to Saudi Arabia and

1. Jami' al Kabir (Great Mosque)
2. Mosque of Salah ad Din (Saladin)
3. Mosque of Al Bakiliya
4. Mosque of Al Madrasa
5. Mosque of Mahdi 'Abbas
6. Mosque of Al Abhar
7. Mosque of Al Mutawakkil
8. Principal sūqs
9. Harat an Nahrein
10. The Imam's palace
11. Burjet Sherāra (open space)
12. Gateway to palace precincts
13. Solbi (open space in Jewish Quarter)
14. Ground formerly excavated for brickmaking material.
15. Gate to Jewish Quarter

This map, drawn by British cartographers in 1946, is of the Yemeni capital, Sanaa. Sanaa, a former capital of the Sabaean Empire, retains its original mud-brick walls, as well as a variety of multilevel stone and brick structures in the old town. The palace of the imam and Islamic mosques, madrasas (schools), and souks (markets), which arrived later, can also be seen on this map.

an undeclared desert border that stretched from Najran to the Omani border in the east.

New Leader, Old Problems

While Yahya was unifying the north, the British, who had been operating freely in the south, were allowing rival groups unlimited access to southern port cities like Aden. In 1948, a group led by Sayyid Abdullah al-Wazzir succeeded in assassinating Yahya. Power stayed with his family, however, as Yahya's oldest son, Ahmad, assumed the leadership and exiled his father's killers. He

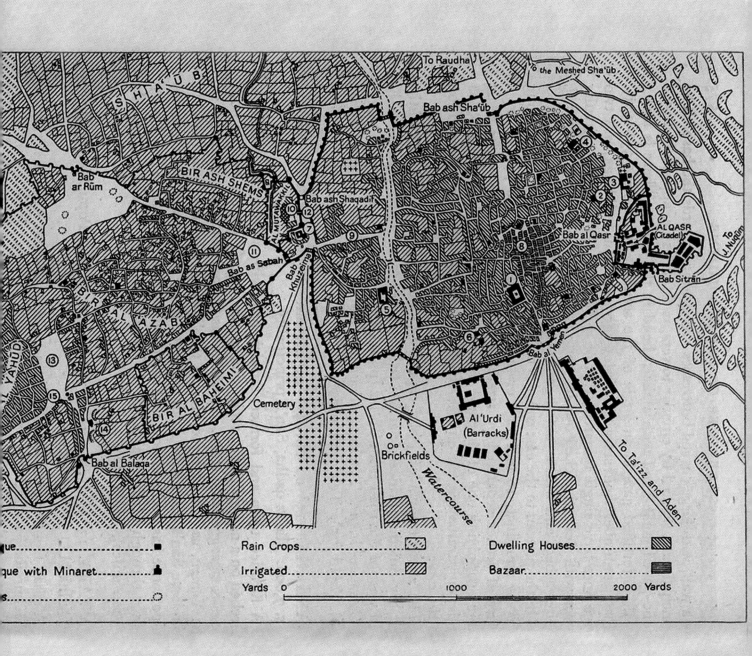

promptly moved the imamate's capital from Sanaa to Ta'izz.

In the years under Yahya, Yemen was largely isolated from other countries. Yahya promoted a state of self-sufficiency because of the country's rich agricultural economy at the time. The rest of the Arab world was modernizing rapidly. Compared to this outside growth, Yemen remained underdeveloped. To improve North Yemen, Ahmad actively sought foreign aid opportunities and established diplomatic relations with countries such as Great Britain, the United States, Egypt, and the Soviet Union.

Despite Ahmad's efforts, the Yemeni imamate remained underdeveloped. Nearly fifteen years after Ahmad came to power, there were no paved roads in North Yemen. Much of its population was in need of medical care. Less than one-fifth of its children had access to a formal education. Ahmad's attempts to industrialize North Yemen had failed.

Border disputes were also increasing. This time, however, the border issues were between Yemen and the British-controlled Aden Protectorate. In desperate need of help, Ahmad turned to Egypt in 1958. These negotiations resulted in Yemen's brief inclusion in the United Arab States. This political union included Yemen and the United Arab Republic (UAR), a merger of Egypt and Syria. This alliance crumbled in 1961.

The Yemen Arab Republic

Imam Ahmad died in September 1962. His son, Crown Prince Mohammed al-Badr, succeeded his father but was deposed after only one week. This removal occurred when an army colonel named Ali Abdullah Saleh incited a revolution. With military support provided by the UAR, Saleh took control. He declared himself president and founded the Yemen Arab Republic (YAR), or North Yemen. The YAR was defined as the area of modern Yemen that is bounded on the west by the Red Sea, in the south and southwest by South Yemen, and in the north by Saudi Arabia. Less than one year after it was created, both the United States and the Soviet Union recognized the YAR. It became a member of the United Nations in 1963.

Life inside Yemen was chaotic in the years that followed its formation. The deposed Mohammed al-Badr fled to the northern mountains. After gaining support from Great Britain and Saudi Arabia, he returned to begin an eight-year civil

Protesters in the British-controlled Aden Protectorate in South Yemen assemble in March 1967 to demand its inclusion in the United Arab States. Some carry posters of Egyptian president Gamal Abdel Nasser, symbolic of the people's support of a foreign leader who had given financial and diplomatic assistance to North Yemen. British troops often clashed with South Yemen's protesters, especially near the border between North and South Yemen.

war. Saleh's republican forces, in contrast, had the support of Egypt and the Soviet Union.

By the time the civil war ended in 1970, President Saleh was exiled to Iraq and al-Badr to Great Britain. The intense fighting had killed nearly 4 percent of the North Yemeni population as well as some 20,000 Egyptian troops. Afterward,

control went to President Qadi Abd al-Rahman al-Iryani and General Hassan al-Amri.

General al-Amri sought to create peace with the remaining forces. Tribe by tribe and with the help of the Saudis, he was successful. In 1970, Saudi Arabia joined the group of countries that recognized the Yemen Arab Republic.

5 SOUTH YEMEN

Yemen Arab Republic (North Yemen)

Sanaa ○

Red Sea

ETHIOPIA

Aden ——————

South Yemen was a colony of the British Crown in 1937, known as the Protectorate of South Arabia. This designation came after a century of rule by British India. The British, in addition to providing protection from the Turkish Ottoman forces in the north, implemented changes that transformed the port city of Aden into a trading hub.

There were thirty-one small sultanates that comprised the Protectorate of South Arabia. The British, however, were concerned with little outside of Aden. The rest of what was to become South Yemen served the British primarily as a buffer against threats from the north. British rulers became involved in daily life only to settle local power struggles or to protect the sultanates during border disputes with North Yemen.

In the 1950s, life became violent in South Yemen as a nationalist spirit emerged throughout

This map illustrates the border between British-controlled South Yemen (known as the People's Democratic Republic of Yemen after 1967) and the Yemen Arab Republic, or North Yemen. Life in South Yemen became increasingly chaotic under the British, as its leaders cared about little more than protecting the port city of Aden. Watching developments in the north, the people of South Yemen wanted to remove the British from power and actively sought to eliminate their presence. To complicate matters, some radical groups, such as the Front for the Liberation of South Yemen (FLOSY), gained financial support from foreign leaders such as Egyptian president Nasser, who also had an interest in seeing the British removed from the region. Another nationalist group that formed to fight for the independence of South Yemen was known as the National Liberation Front (NLF).

SAUDI ARABIA

PEOPLE'S DEMOCRATIC REPUBLIC OF YEMEN
(SouthYemen)

Gulf of Aden

the region. Strikes against British rule occurred frequently. As the 1960s progressed, the absent British rulers had problems maintaining control. In 1963, Britain renamed the Protectorate of South Arabia and it became known as the Aden Protectorate. The new Federation of South Arabia included Aden as a distinct colony. There was opposition to this act, and when the revolution in the north began, the growing nationalist movement was initiated.

South Yemen's strongest nationalist party was the left-wing National Liberation Front (NLF). Spurred on by the revolution in the north, the NLF began a four-year campaign of terror in 1963. The result was complete British withdrawal from Yemen and the dissolution of the federation.

The NLF became the only recognized political party in South Yemen. It was significantly more aggressive than the freedom fighters of the north. The NLF was formed by Marxist and nationalist militants with Qahtan Muhammad al-Shaabi as president. The guerrilla tactics of the NLF and intensity of the fighting

Marxism

Marxism is an economic and political philosophy named for German philosopher Karl Marx (1818–1883). It is also known as scientific socialism. Marxism consisted of three related ideas: a philosophical view of man, a theory of history, and an economic and political program. Modern Communism finds its roots in Marxism. Most socialist theories come from it.

Socialism is a general term for the political and economic theory that advocates a government system of collective ownership and management of the production and distribution of goods. Socialism exists in direct contrast to the Western philosophy of capitalism. Capitalism stresses competition and profit, while socialism calls for cooperation and social service.

Karl Marx (*above*) argued that the conditions of modern industrial societies result in the estrangement of workers from their own labor.

had the British preparing for the independence of South Yemen by 1967. By November, Marxist guerrillas forced the British out of Aden, and the NLF declared the Republic of South Yemen independent.

At the time of its independence, South Yemen was made up of the irregularly shaped southern end of the Arabian Peninsula and some islands in the Arabian Sea. It was defined by unofficial borders with North Yemen, Saudi Arabia, and Oman, as well as a shoreline along the Arabian Sea.

As when North Yemen claimed its independence from the Turks, South Yemen faced similar challenges. Its economy was on the verge of collapse, and its external relationships were strained. Making matters more difficult, the YAR supported the right-wing opposition to the new government. In addition, the closure of the Suez Canal put increased pressure on Aden as a trading port. As a

Above are armed members of the Yemeni National Liberation Front, who forced the British to withdraw in 1967. The federation became independent as the People's Democratic Republic of Yemen (PDRY). Even though the British were expelled, there was hostility with North Yemen, and a hard road followed for the country. Fighting began in 1971 and became open warfare between the two Yemens in October 1972. The Yemen Arab Republic (YAR) received aid from Saudi Arabia and the PDRY was supplied with Soviet arms.

result, South Yemen relied on economic assistance from Communist countries such as the Soviet Union, China, and East Germany. In 1967, South Yemen officially became the People's Democratic Republic of Yemen (PDRY). Not long after, the NLF developed into the Yemeni Socialist Party (YSP).

Politically, the situation started to stabilize in 1969 when Salim 'Ali Rubayyi was appointed president of South Yemen. This act signaled the beginning of the corrective movement. In an effort to combat the crumbling economy, Rubayyi brought it under government control.

Between 1969 and 1978, South Yemen was governed under a constitution administered by the coleadership of Rubayyi and a rival Marxist, 'Abd al-Fattah Isma'il. Both Rubayyi and Isma'il made efforts to organize the country according to their individual versions of Marxism.

Conflict with the North

The initial months of independence were not easy for the PDRY. In addition to economic strain, the new government became embroiled in border disputes with both the YAR and Oman. Some clashes became violent, and a brief conflict erupted in 1972. An accord prompted by the Arab League was signed between the YAR and the PDRY that called for an end to the fighting that same year. It also recommended a merge of North and South Yemen within twelve months. This agreement would not be implemented for several years, and differences continued between North and South Yemen.

This was an effort to rescue his country from a declining infrastructure and political isolation. Isma'il signed a twenty-year treaty with the Soviet Union in 1972. This agreement encouraged greater Soviet involvement in the republic. As the Arab world's only Marxist state, South Yemen stood as a symbol to its Communist partners.

In 1974, YAR president al-Iryani was replaced with Colonel Ibrahim al-Hamdi. Al-Hamdi guided the country toward moderate political beliefs. As a result, external relations with the United States and Saudi Arabia improved. As the PDRY government

At right is a photo taken on October 12, 1977, of Colonel Ibrahim al-Hamdi, the president of North Yemen. Al-Hamdi was president from 1974 to 1977. Among his most important reforms was replacing many of the 3,000 army officers, many illiterate tribal chiefs, with young and educated military personnel. Al-Hamdi introduced reforms that made him unpopular among tribal chiefs. He managed to improve relations with South Yemen and the Soviet Union but was assassinated in 1977, two days before leaving for South Yemen to sign a mutual defense pact. It was widely thought that Saudi activists were behind the killing.

continued to move farther left toward Marxism, external relationships with other countries, including the one between the two Yemens, worsened. It would take another two years before South Yemen's conflicts subsided. By 1976, many of the hostilities with Oman had ended, and Saudi Arabia again recognized the government of South Yemen.

As the 1970s ended, political change was happening on both sides of the violet line. In the north, President al-Hamdi was assassinated. His successor, Colonel Ahmad ibn Hussein al-Ghashmi, ruled for less than a year before he, too, was killed. Politically, the situation was much the same in the south. In 1978, Rubayyi was deposed and executed, presumably for ordering the assassination of al-Ghashmi. Rubayyi's rival, 'Abd al-Fattah Isma'il, replaced him.

These political upheavals again led to violence. By 1979, fighting had broken out between North and South Yemen. Yet the fighting was stopped within one month with another peace treaty.

6 A UNIFIED NATION

In the 1980s, both the YAR and the PDRY were recovering from a state of instability. This was caused by a seemingly endless succession of leaders. The YAR achieved some degree of stability under the presidency of Lieutenant Colonel Ali Abdullah Saleh. Saleh embraced a Western-style economy, and under his leadership, the country's economy grew. However, the path toward a stable YAR was difficult. Rebellions against Saleh's government raged in 1981 and 1982. These were spurred on by a coalition of Islamic forces and PDRY dissidents.

By the mid-1980s, conflicts between internal groups had been contained. Political parties were outlawed, and the military was in control of government positions. Saleh was elected president three times. He helped to maintain stable relationships—internally and externally—by carefully selecting his government's ministers and tribal representatives.

Saleh's government turned the YAR into a modern nation within the span of fifteen years. It can be argued that his success was due to the willingness of the population to experience change. Even though South Yemen was then a devoutly Islamic country, North Yemen readily adopted some Western attitudes.

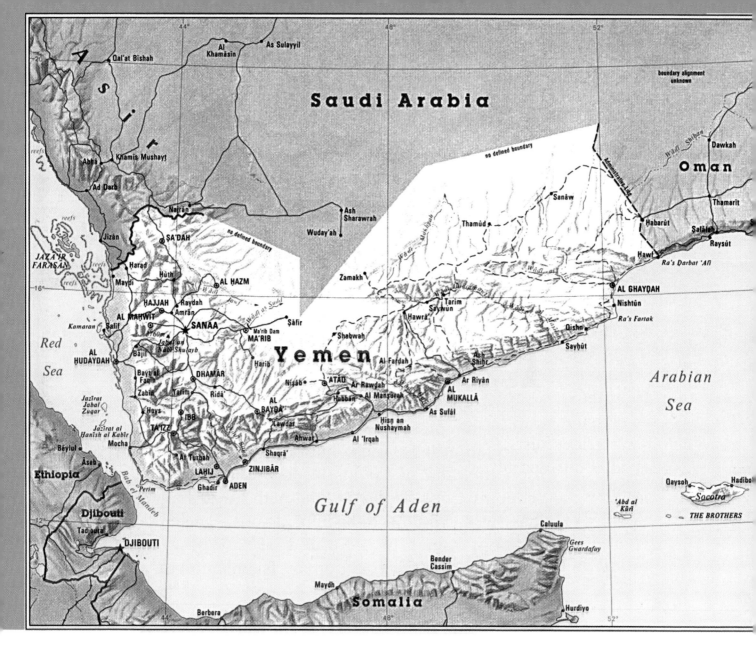

Qal'at Bishah
Al Khamāsin
As Sulayyil

boundary alignment unknown

Dawkah

Oman

Abhā
Khamis Mushayṭ

Ad Darb

Najrān

Thamarīt
Ḥabarūt

Ṣanāw

no defined boundary

Thamūd

Salālah

Jizān
SA'DAH
no defined boundary

Ash Sharawrah
Wuday'ah

Raysūt

Ḥawf
Ra's Darbat 'Alī

JAZĀ'IR FARASĀN
reefs

Harad
Hūth

Zamakh

AL GHAYDAH

Maydī
AL ḤAZM

Nishṭūn

HAJJAH
Raydah
Amrān

Şāfir

Tarim
Say'wun

Ra's Fartak

AL MAHWIT
Kamarān
Salif
SANAA
MA'RIB
Ma'rib Dam

Hawrā

Qishn

Shabwah

Ash Shihr

Sayḥūt

Red Sea
AL ḤUDAYDAH
Bājil
Jabal an Nabī Shu'ayb

Harib

Yemen

Al Fardah

AL MUKALLĀ

Arabian Sea

Bayt al Faqīh
Zabīd

DHAMĀR

Nisāb
ATAQ
Ar Rawdah

Ḥabbān
Al Manṣūrah
AL

Ar Riyān

Jazirat Jabal Zuqar
Hays
IBB
Rida'
AL BAYDA'

As Sufāl

Jazirat al Hanīsh al Kabīr
TA'IZZ
Lawdar
Hisn an Nushaymah

Béylul
Mocha
Al Turbah

Ahwar
Al 'Irqah

'Abd al Kūrī
Qaysoh
Hadibo

Āseb
Ghadir
LAHIJ
ADEN
Shaqrā'
ZINJIBĀR

Socotra
THE BROTHERS

Ethiopia
Perim
Bab el Mandeb

Gulf of Aden

Caluula

Djibouti
Tadjoura

Gees Gwardafuy

DJIBOUTI

Bender Cassim

Maydh

Hurdiyo

Somalia

Berbera

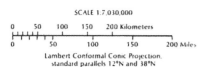

International boundary
★ National capital
⊚ Governorate capital
Railroad
Road
Track

SCALE 1:7,030,000

0   50   100   150   200 Kilometers

0   50   100   150   200 Miles

Lambert Conformal Conic Projection,
standard parallels 12°N and 38°N

This map, drawn in the 1990s by the U.S. Central Intelligence Agency, shows the former independent states of North and South Yemen united as one country, the Republic of Yemen. This union took place in 1990 after wars between the two countries in 1972 and 1979. Ali Abdullah Saleh, former leader of North Yemen, was the first president of the Republic of Yemen and Sanaa was declared its national capital.

Ongoing Struggles

The people of the PDRY did not find stability as quickly. The YSP was in power with a platform that was more leftist than most of the world's Communist countries. During the 1970s, the PDRY government offered asylum to Palestinian hijackers as well as extreme left-wing terrorist groups. This action so outraged Western powers that many countries, including the United States, refused to establish relations with the PDRY.

After the 1979 war ended, 'Ali Nasir Muhammad formally replaced PDRY president Isma'il, who went into exile in Moscow. Gradually, Muhammad opened the south to the outside world, focusing on building relationships with other Arab countries. Muhammad remained true, however, to the country's strong socialist doctrine. Clashes between the government and extreme Marxists increased. In 1986, Isma'il returned, and a bloody civil war followed.

Beginning in Aden, and resulting in the deaths of thousands of PDRY citizens, the 1986 civil war brought another change in leadership to South Yemen. Isma'il was dead and 'Ali Nasir Muhammad fled to Ethiopia. A new president, Haydar Abu Bakr al-'Attas, was chosen. He flew to Aden from Communist Moscow to become head of state.

International Impact

Changes in the global political landscape, specifically the collapse of the Soviet Union, also played a role in the eventual unification of the two Yemens. As the 1980s ended, the alliance between the PDRY and Gorbachev's Soviet Union faltered. The Soviet economy slowed and so did financial aid into South Yemen, which was facing bankruptcy.

It did not take the nervous southern government long to realize that its strict socialist stance and extreme left-wing policies left it with few friends outside the Communist bloc.

This photo of former Soviet president Mikhail Gorbachev was taken in 1996. Gorbachev resigned as president when the Soviet Union disintegrated in December 1991. In 1992, he became the head of the Foundation for Social, Economic, and Political Research, a think tank that was founded after the breakup of the USSR.

In the final analysis, the PDRY had little choice but to turn to its Yemeni brothers in the YAR for help.

It is important to note that unification talks were not unusual between North and South Yemen. It had become commonplace to issue declarations of friendship and peace between the two nations. However, in the late 1980s, there were many reasons why these talks were taken more seriously. The PDRY was in a desperate economic situation. Yemeni people on both sides of the border wanted to be unified. In

addition, Western oil companies had discovered considerable oil deposits in the desert area on both sides of the violet line. Now unification was an economic necessity.

One Voice Rises

By the late 1980s, the YAR and PDRY faced a monumental decision. There were two options: They could continue to argue over rights to the recently discovered oil reserves, or they could formalize the border, form a neutral zone, and use the once-disputed area cooperatively. In

On October 6, 2002, there was an explosion on the French oil tanker *Limberg*. The ship was attacked by a small boat that had explosives on it and caught fire off the coast of Yemen. In the photo above, Yemeni soldiers stand guard on the beach at Mukalla in Yemen, 480 miles (772 km) south of Sanaa. Spots of oil still appeared on the surface of the beach on October 8. The Yemeni government asked the Canadian oil firm Nexen Inc. to help clean up the oil spill after the blast.

Oil and Gas Reserves

Though the discovery of oil and natural gas reserves proved to be a turning point for many Middle Eastern countries in the 1980s, this has not been the case with Yemen.

The search for oil had proved fruitless until 1984, when oil was actively found and exported from Yemen. With violent border disputes between North and South Yemen as well as with Saudi Arabia, it was difficult for international developers to build a reliable oil business in this politically unstable country.

Today, the country's oil reserves are centered in five main areas: Mar'ib-Jawf in the north, East Shabwah and Masila in the south, and Jannah and Lyad in central Yemen. The Masila block is the country's most productive oil field. Yemen's considerable natural gas reserves are located primarily in the Mar'ib-Jawf.

May 1988, leaders from both countries agreed to cooperate. By November 1989, the two governments had outlined a plan to unite North and South Yemen.

Not everyone wanted the two countries to unite. Between the 1989 promise of unity and the May 22, 1990, emergence of the unified Republic of Yemen, opposition was waged. In the north, the religious elite were vehemently opposed to a unified state. They used northern mosques to spread propaganda about South Yemen; they called it an unruly society where women left their faces unveiled and men roamed the streets.

Outside the country, the greatest voice of opposition to unification came from the Saudis. Since the 1984 discovery of oil, the Yemeni economy had become increasingly independent. As a result, Saudi Arabia lost considerable influence over its southern neighbor. In addition, YAR oil production enabled it to join with Jordan, Egypt, and Iraq in the Arab Cooperative Council (ACC). The ACC was a group of member nations united to promote unity in the Arab region. This coalition greatly weakened Saudi Arabia's power on the peninsula.

Although the ACC no longer existed in 1990, a unified Yemen also presented a security nightmare for Saudi Arabia. Together, the two Yemens would boast a greater population than Saudi Arabia. Yemen would also control enough oil reserves to make economic independence possible. And, perhaps most important, a unified Yemen would be the only country on the Arabian Peninsula to have direct access to the Red and Arabian Seas.

7 THE REPUBLIC OF YEMEN

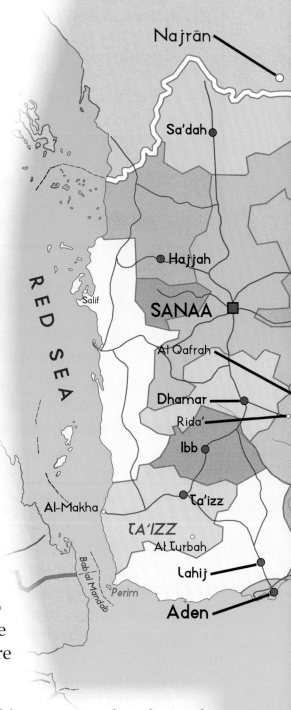

Fortunately for Yemen, opposition to unity did not prevail. By 1990, the PDRY and the YAR were unwilling to wait any longer to unite. The disputed border was defined, demilitarized, and opened. Individual state security forces were dissolved. Free enterprise was legalized in the PDRY as were political parties in the YAR. Existing currencies were made valid in both countries. On May 22, 1990, the Republic of Yemen emerged.

Sanaa became the capital of the new country. YAR president Saleh became president of the unified Yemen. Ali Salim al-Bidh was installed as vice president. PDRY president Haydar Abu Bakr al-'Attas took the position of prime minister.

Unfortunately, the peace that appeared to resolve a bitter divide would be short-lived. The first few years in newly unified Yemen were flawed by trouble.

The United Republic of Yemen is shown on this contemporary map of the country. Since the unification of Yemen in 1990, disagreements between northern and southern leaders have erupted and threatened to again divide the country. In 1994, a short but violent civil war took place in Yemen when southern leaders attempted to break away from the country. They were quickly controlled by troops from the north. Although Yemen has a dramatic and divided past, its president, Ali Abdullah Saleh, hopes that the country and its leaders will remain united.

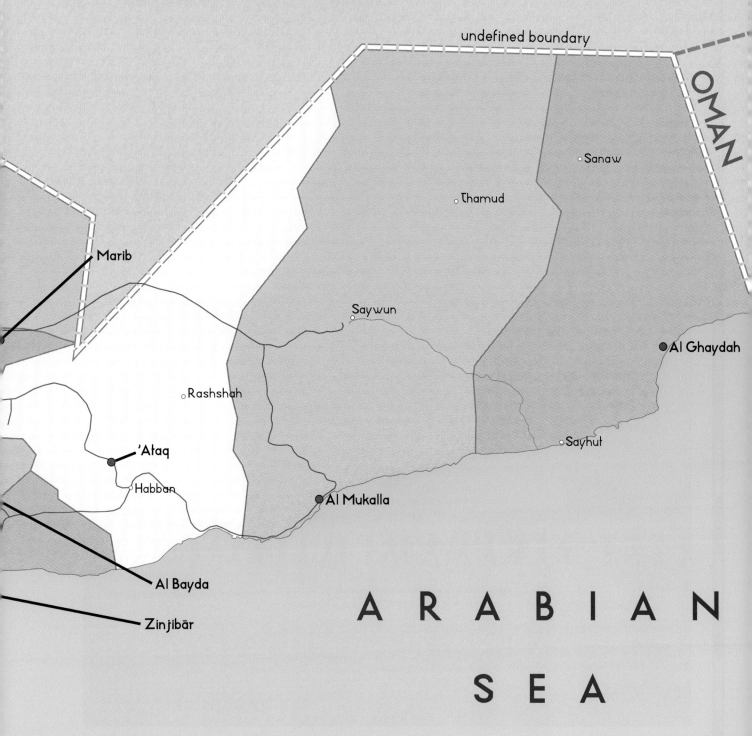

SAUDI ARABIA

undefined boundary

OMAN

Sanaw

Thamud

Marib

Saywun

Al Ghaydah

Rashshah

'Ataq

Sayhut

Habban

Al Mukalla

Al Bayda

Zinjibār

A R A B I A N

S E A

Gulf of Aden

A Rocky Start

Just three months after Yemeni uni-fication, conflict erupted in the Middle East. Iraqi president Saddam Hussein invaded and occu-pied neighboring Kuwait. Although not directly involved in this action, Yemen took a moderate stand, favoring an "Arab solution to an Arab problem." President Saleh demanded the withdrawal of Iraqi troops from Kuwait. He also wanted Western forces out of Saudi Arabia, as did other Arab nations. The West criticized Yemen's state-ments as well, viewing them as a sign of alliance with Iraq. The antic-ipated benefits of unification were already overshadowed.

Internally, Yemen's economic conditions were worsening. The sudden influx of Yemeni emigrants from Saudi Arabia—a result of Yemen's statements regarding Kuwait—brought the newly unified

Sadayuki Mikami took this photo of a line of captured Iraqi soldiers marching through the Kuwait desert during the Persian Gulf War on Sunday morning, February 24, 1991. These soldiers are being guarded by vehicles of the U.S. Marine Second Division. The Second Division was located just west of several mine-fields in the desert. A cease-fire would take place on February 28, 1991, and by June, there would be a United States "victory parade" in Washington, D.C.

nation to the brink of collapse. The stress of a failing economy caused friction between ruling parties, and as the elections approached, violence erupted. Many YSP officials were assassinated, but Saleh's government made no attempts to punish the assassins.

With the thirty-month term of the provisional constitution winding down, Yemen held democratic elections for the first time in May 1993. Saleh, who had been appointed pres-

ident in 1990, was opposed in the election by his vice president, Ali Salim al-Bidh. Saleh was reelected in 1993, and political tensions increased. Al-Bidh refused to return to Sanaa after the elections or to participate in the government. Although the Yemeni people embraced democracy, the leadership was not ready to.

Civil War

Integrating the two Yemeni governments had proved more difficult

Photographer Patrick Robert took this photo on July 6, 1994, in Aden, Yemen, during the civil war taking place between the "two Yemens," as they were called at the time. Southern Yemeni leaders' demand for secession led to the brief civil war. The government tried to maintain unity, but it had to deal with ongoing intratribal warfare. There were also kidnappings and other acts of sabotage committed by local extremists. Since the civil war, Yemen has had disputes with Eritrea over the Hanish Islands in the Red Sea and with Saudi Arabia over islands to the north.

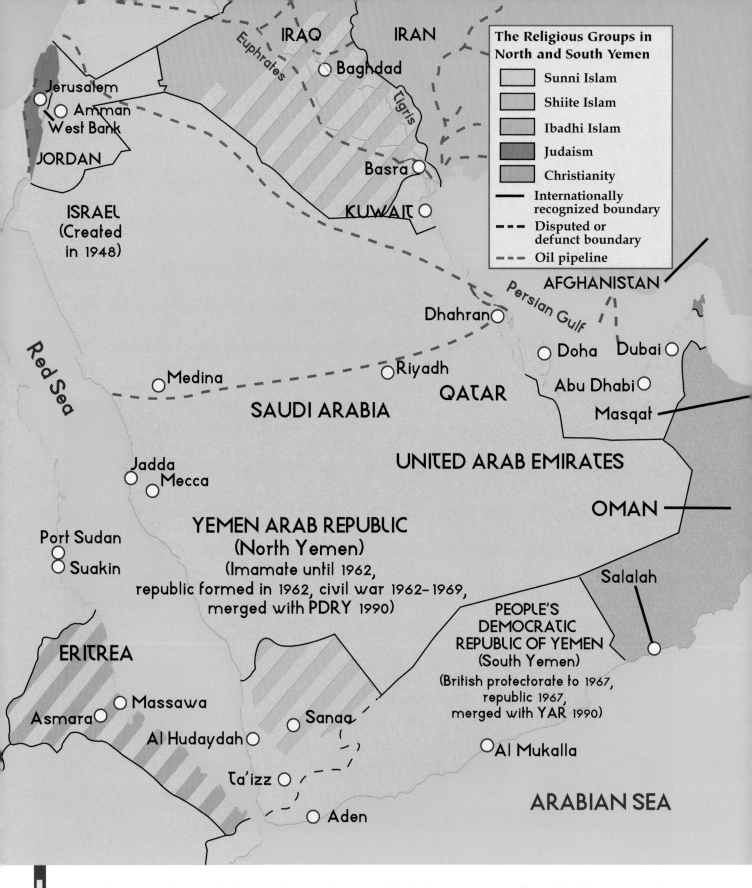

The Religious Groups in North and South Yemen

- Sunni Islam
- Shiite Islam
- Ibadhi Islam
- Judaism
- Christianity

—— Internationally recognized boundary

- - - Disputed or defunct boundary

– · – Oil pipeline

Jerusalem
Amman
West Bank
JORDAN
ISRAEL (Created in 1948)

IRAQ
Euphrates
Baghdad
Tigris
Basra
KUWAIT

IRAN

AFGHANISTAN

Dhahran
Persian Gulf
Doha
Dubai
Abu Dhabi
Masqat
QATAR
Medina
Riyadh
SAUDI ARABIA

Red Sea

UNITED ARAB EMIRATES

OMAN

Jadda
Mecca

Port Sudan
Suakin

YEMEN ARAB REPUBLIC
(North Yemen)
(Imamate until 1962,
republic formed in 1962, civil war 1962–1969,
merged with PDRY 1990)

Salalah

PEOPLE'S
DEMOCRATIC
REPUBLIC OF YEMEN
(South Yemen)
(British protectorate to 1967,
republic 1967,
merged with YAR 1990)

ERITREA

Massawa
Asmara

Al Hudaydah
Sanaa

Al Mukalla

Ta'izz

Aden

ARABIAN SEA

Differences in religious ideology, as shown on this map of divided Yemen, continually troubled the country after civil infighting was stopped and Yemen again became united in 1994. Conflicts continued between leaders in the north, which is more religiously conservative, and in the south, where leaders are more liberal.

than had been anticipated. Divided loyalties eventually led to a fierce civil war that began on May 4, 1994. On May 21, southern leaders declared secession from the republic and established the Democratic Republic of Yemen (DRY).

Almost all of the fighting during the war took place in the south. Southern forces sought support from neighboring states and were successful in securing billions of dollars in assistance. The international community refused to recognize this new secessionist state, however. Much of the support the revolutionaries had before the war broke out disappeared.

Unfortunately for the secessionists, it would seem their fate was predetermined. Aden was surrounded by northern forces in less than twenty days. The powerful southern leader al-Bidh fled to Al Mukalla in Hadhramaut to escape the fighting.

Aden finally fell to Saleh's northern forces on July 7, 1994. Other resistance groups quickly collapsed, and thousands of southern leaders went into exile. In order to avoid imprisonment, al-Bidh was granted asylum in Oman under the condition that he permanently retire from politics.

The Aftermath

Though the war reinforced the desire of the common people for

Thomas Hartwell took this photo of the president of North Yemen, Ali Abdullah Saleh, attending the Arab League summit in 1989. There was an assassination attempt on Saleh in May 2000 on the eve of Yemen's tenth anniversary unity celebration. Six people attempted to ambush the president in Sanaa. They were apprehended.

Yemeni unification, troubles for the new nation did not end. Inflation was rampant. Conflicts between the more secular south and the conservative north continued. Intermittent border skirmishes with Saudi Arabia also destabilized the country. Assassination attempts and the kidnapping of foreigners and several prominent Yemenis plagued the country. The ongoing unrest had stopped the return of tourists, international investment, and economic development.

In September 1994, major reforms to the country's 1991 constitution were ratified. In October of that same year, Saleh was reelected president. He appointed Abd-Rabbuh Mansur Hadi as vice president. In order to revive Yemen's ailing economy, the leaders implemented an economic austerity (thrift) program the following year.

In February 1995, Saleh and King Fahd of Saudi Arabia looked to bring an end to their border disputes. They agreed to negotiate as skirmishes were still taking place. It was generally agreed that the mere prospect of an end to the fighting was enough to prevent additional battles. It took five years, but in June 2000, Yemen and Saudi Arabia jointly announced an agreement that ended their sixty-six-year border controversy.

Unfortunately for Yemen, resolving the Saudi border issue would

This photo taken on May 22, 2000, shows the Yemeni president Ali Abdullah Saleh (bottom left) watching a military parade. The parade marked the tenth anniversary of the unification of North and South Yemen. Saudi crown prince Abdullah bin Abdel Aziz (bottom right) sits with his delegation. Crown Prince Abdullah bin Abdel Aziz traveled to Russia in September 2003 to make the first high-level visit to Russia from his kingdom. The mission was to strengthen cooperation between the two countries in oil and gas investment. After Saudi Arabia, Russia is the second biggest oil exporter in the world.

not end its territory issues. Also in 1995, Eritrea—an independent African nation that lies across the Red Sea from Yemen—seized the Hanish Islands, located at the mouth of the Red Sea. Eritrean troops attacked Yemeni troops stationed on the island, killing twelve. In 1996, the two nations agreed to negotiations related to sovereignty over the islands. The Eritrean troops withdrew. Two years later, in October

In 1995, people from Eritrea, a country that gained its independence from Ethiopia in 1993, seized Hanish al Kabir (Greater Hanish Island), an island situated strategically at the mouth of the Red Sea. At least a dozen people were killed during the conflict, which lasted until the following year. After the two nations submitted to a diplomatic review over which one legally held dominion over the island, it was decided that it belonged to Yemen.

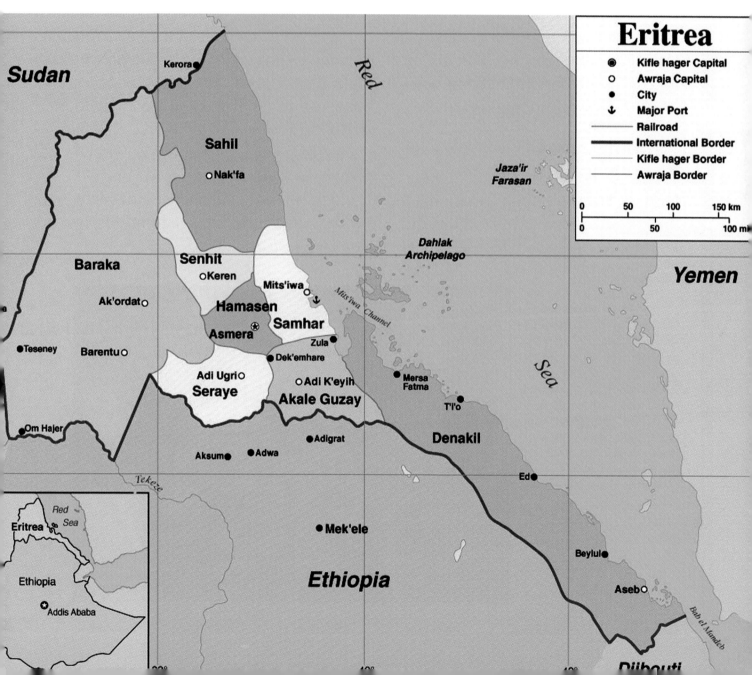

1998, both countries accepted the decision reached by the international arbitration panel that granted Yemen dominion over the Hanish Islands.

As the twenty-first century approached, the stage in Yemen was set for improving international relations. Unfortunately, the country's legacy of international isolation and internal mistrust has prevented unified Yemen from capitalizing on many of its strengths, specifically its strategic location and the oil and natural gas reserves that could lead to its economic independence.

United States–Yemen Relations

United States–Yemen relations go back to the early days of the republic. Stable despite many significant political events, the relationship between the two nations has positively influenced Yemeni society. The continuing cooperation between Yemen and the United States can be illustrated by the 1998 formation of the Fulbright Alumni Association of Yemen (FAAY) and the 1999 Yemeni-American Medical Conference. In 1999, a meeting between U.S. general Tommy Franks, commander of the American Special Forces, and Yemen's government officials resulted in a joint de-mining process of areas in Yemen that are riddled with land mines.

Perhaps the most controversial area surrounding United States–Yemen relations has been in the area of security related to the bombing of the USS *Cole* in 2000.

In this photo, U.S. general Tommy Franks, commander of U.S. Central Command, speaks at a press conference in Sanaa, Yemen, on October 17, 2002. Franks talked about several patrol boats that were donated to the Yemeni coast guard from the United States government. Franks also discussed the need for Yemen's cooperation with America on the "war on terror."

Ties to Terrorism

Despite successful international alliances with Arab and Western nations, Yemen has been fraught with reports of terrorist activities and ties to terrorist organizations. These rumblings sometimes overshadow positive momentum in international relationships. In 1998, for example, a group of Islamic militants in Yemen kidnapped a number of foreigners. These kidnappings culminated in December 1998 when four tourists were killed during a failed rescue attempt by Yemeni forces. As recently as 2000, a Norwegian diplomat was killed by gunfire after being kidnapped.

On October 12, 2000, terrorist activities in Yemen took another turn as the USS *Cole*, a U.S. Navy destroyer, was deliberately bombed while refueling in the waters off the coast of Aden. The attack killed seventeen Americans and injured thirty-nine others.

Above, the USS *Cole* is towed by the Military Sealift Command tug USNS *Catawba* on Sunday, October 29, 2000, after a bomb struck the *Cole* on October 12. The bomb, detonated by two suicide bombers who pulled up alongside the *Cole*, killed seventeen crew members and injured thirty-nine. The *Cole* was then lifted aboard the Norwegian transport ship the *Blue Marlin* and taken back to the United States. It took about five weeks for the damaged destroyer to return. The USS *Cole* was in a Yemen port when it was bombed. Yemeni officials said they would cooperate to the best of their abilities to find the organization that masterminded the bombing.

American officials suspected that Saudi exile Osama bin Laden was linked to the attack. Eventually, suspects in the bombing—including Yemeni nationals—were arrested in Yemen and Pakistan.

Yemeni nationals have been linked to terrorist activities. Yet the Yemeni foreign minister has said that cooperation between the United States and Yemen is "at its best in the area of combating terrorism." Referring to the United States as a "friend and partner in facing the current challenge [of] terrorism," the foreign minister declared that the "incident of the *Cole* has strengthened relations with the United States." He indicated in an interview with the *Yemen Times* in April 2001 that actions taken after the attack "made clear to the Americans that Yemen and President Saleh will not hesitate to take firm action against terrorism in the country."

An International Alliance

The Yemeni government was also publicly allied with the United States in the war against terrorism in 2001. Early in the morning on September 11, terrorists hijacked three passenger planes from airports in Boston, Newark, and in Washington, D.C., and deliberately crashed them into the twin towers of the World Trade Center in New York City and the Pentagon, near Washington, D.C. A fourth hijacked plane crashed into a field outside of Pittsburgh, Pennsylvania. It was widely accepted that Osama bin Laden and the terrorist organization Al Qaeda were responsible. It was also known that many of the Arab fighters who supported these groups originated in Yemen.

In the wake of these attacks, the Yemeni government cooperated with U.S. investigators. It arrested a number of Muslim extremists. It also launched a military offensive against the factions of bin Laden's Al Qaeda terrorist network operating within Yemen. In November 2001, Saleh met with U.S. president George W. Bush to repeat his commitment to support the United States. Also on the agenda was a proposed package of U.S. aid to Yemen worth as much as $400 million.

Evidence presented in February 2002 linked two of the suspects in the USS *Cole* bombing to the September 11 attacks. It also linked them to a plot to bomb the U.S. Embassy in Sanaa. In response, the Yemeni government agreed to the deployment of U.S. military advisers to Yemen. The balance of the year saw significant advances in the fight against terror as a top Al Qaeda

Photographer Bryant Macdougall took this photo of men at a newspaper stand in Sanaa, Yemen, on Tuesday, November 5, 2002. They are reading about an explosion in Marib the day before in which six suspected Al Qaeda operatives were killed when the CIA launched a Hellfire missile at their vehicle. Eventually, news from officials in Yemen declared that one of the passengers was Qaed Salim Sinan al-Harethi, one of Osama bin Laden's top lieutenants in Yemen, suspected to have led the attack on the USS *Cole*.

leader was killed in Yemen and a ship containing scud missiles en route to Yemen from North Korea was seized.

Opportunities

What the future holds for Yemen is unknown. In 2003, Yemen was facing tremendous internal struggles regarding the decision to join the World Trade Organization (WTO). This is an international body that promotes and enforces the provisions of trade laws and regulations. Full membership, anticipated to be in place by 2005, would bring unprecedented competition to the local economy.

As a new democracy with authority over substantial natural gas and oil reserves, Yemen is home to what is arguably one of the most diverse cultural, religious, and ecological landscapes in the Middle East.

TIMELINE

1200 BC–AD 525 South Arabian kingdoms of Sheba, Ma'in, Qataban, and Hadhramaut flourish.

700 BC Great dam at Marib constructed.

Late AD 200s Himyarite rule unites South Arabia under one ruler.

570 The dam at Marib collapses.

575 Sassanid Empire conquers Sabaean kingdom.

628 Yemeni people embrace Islam.

661–822 Yemen is under the control of Muslim caliphs.

819 Ziyad dynasty comes to power in southern Yemen.

Late 800s Zaydi imamate founded in northern Yemen.

1138–1446 Yemen controlled by series of Sunni dynasties.

1517–1636 First Ottoman rule in southern and southeastern Yemen.

1618 British establish coffee trading center in Mocha (Al-Makha).

1658 All of Yemen united under Himyarite rule.

1839 British seize Aden and lay foundation for formation of the Protectorate of South Arabia.

1872–1923 Second period of Ottoman rule in Yemen.

1934 Saudi-Yemeni War occurs—the first major border dispute.

1962 Yemen Arab Republic (North Yemen) becomes independent.

1967 South Yemen becomes the People's Democratic Republic of Yemen.

1979 A war occurs between North and South Yemen.

1984 Gas and oil deposits are discovered in Yemen.

1986 A civil war occurs in People's Democratic Republic of Yemen.

1990 North and South Yemen formally unite as the Republic of Yemen.

1991 A new constitution for the unified Yemen is approved.

1993 Parliamentary elections take place for the first time.

1994 Another civil war takes place.

1995 Eritrea invades Hanish Islands in the Red Sea. Three-year sovereignty debate begins.

1997 Second general parliamentary elections.

1998 Sovereignty over Hanish Islands granted to Yemen.

2000 The USS *Cole* is attacked. The first presidential election is held. Yemeni-Saudi border dispute is successfully arbitrated.

2001 Wahiba Fare is the first woman appointed in the Yemeni cabinet as minister of state for human rights. Yemeni president Saleh visits United States and requests support for fighting terrorist elements in Yemen.

2002 Yemen expels more than 100 scholars suspected of supporting the Al Qaeda terrorist organization.

2003 Yemeni nationals suspected of orchestrating the bombing of the USS *Cole* escape Yemeni prison. Parliamentary elections are held.

GLOSSARY

Aden The port and second largest city of Yemen; former British colony.

Arab A member of a group of Semitic Arabic-speaking peoples who live throughout North Africa and the Middle East.

asylum The protection from arrest and extradition given to political refugees by a nation or embassy.

Christianity The religion based on the life, teachings, and example of Jesus Christ.

coalition A temporary union between two or more political parties.

dissident A person who publicly disagrees with an established political or religious system or organization.

frankincense An aromatic gum or resin often burned as incense.

Himyarite A member of an ancient people who lived in southern parts of the Arabian Peninsula.

imam The leader of an Islamic community.

imamate The area in which an imam is leader.

incense A substance that is burned for its fragrant aroma.

Islam The religion of Muslims, based upon the teachings of the prophet Muhammad.

Koran The sacred text of Islam, believed by Muslims to record the revelations of Allah to Muhammad.

left A political viewpoint categorized by the desire to reform the government in order to advocate change in the name of greater freedom or well-being of the common man; opposite of the right, a conservative political viewpoint.

Levant The region on the eastern shore of the Mediterranean Sea that historically extended from Greece to Egypt.

Marxism A political ideology based on the theories of Karl Marx.

Minaean A member of a Semitic people who ruled part of southern Arabia from 1200 to 650 BC.

monotheism The belief that there is only one god.

Muslim A person who believes in and follows the teachings of Islam.

myrrh An aromatic resin used in perfume, incense, and medicinal preparations.

polytheism The belief in several deities.

qat A plant grown in Yemen that contains chemicals that produce a lucid dreamlike state and feelings of energy and euphoria.

Sanaa The political capital of Yemen, revered by many Arabs as the birthplace of the Arab civilization.

Shia The branch of Islam that considers Ali, the cousin of Muhammad, and his descendants as Muhammad's true successors.

socialism A political system of communal ownership.

Sunni A sect of Islam that supports the traditional method of election to the caliphate.

terrorism The use of violence or the threat of violence to create fear or alarm. Terrorism is often carried out for political purposes. The word "terrorism" first appeared during the French Revolution (1789–1799) to describe the practice of some revolutionaries.

wadi A steep-sided watercourse in which water flows only after heavy rainfalls.

welfare state A nation whose government assumes primary responsibility for the social welfare of its citizens.

FOR MORE INFORMATION

Embassy of the Republic of Yemen
2600 Virginia Avenue NW, Suite 705
Washington, DC 20037
(202) 965-4760
Web site: http://www.
yemenembassy.org

Web Sites

Due to the changing nature of Internet links, the Rosen Publishing Group, Inc., has developed an online list of Web sites related to the subject of this book. This site is updated regularly. Please use this link to access the list:

http://www.rosenlinks.com/liha/yeme

FOR FURTHER READING

Hestler, Anna. *Yemen* (Cultures of the World). New York: Benchmark Books, 1999.
Searight, Sandra. *Yemen: Land and People*. London: Pallas Athene Publishing, 2002.

Wald, Peter. *Yemen* (Pallas Guide Series). London: Cimino Publishing Group, 2002.
Weber, Sandra. *Yemen* (Creation of the Middle East). Broomall, PA: Chelsea House, 2002.

BIBLIOGRAPHY

Cockburn, Andrew. "Yemen United." *National Geographic*, Vol. 197, No. 4, April 2000, pp. 24–30.
Hamalainen, Pertti. *Yemen*. Hawthorn, Australia: Lonely Planet Publications, 1999.
Hestler, Anna. *Yemen* (Cultures of the World). New York: Benchmark Books, 1999.
"Historical Background." Y.Net: The Main ISP of Yemen. Retrieved March 12, 2003 (http://www.y. net.ye/yemen/hbackground.htm).
Mackintosh-Smith, Tim. *Yemen: The Unknown Arabia*. Woodstock, NY: Overlook Press, 2000.
Nyrop, Richard F., ed. *The Yemens: Country Studies*. Washington, DC:

Foreign Area Studies, The American University, Library of Congress, 1986.
"Republic of Yemen." Microsoft Encarta Online Encyclopedia. 2003. Retrieved March 15, 2003 (http://encarta.msn.com).
"Yemen." The Columbia Electronic Encyclopedia. 2003. Retrieved March 12, 2003 (http://www. 1upinfo.com/encyclopedia/Y/ Yemen.html).
"Yemen History and Government." Worldtravelguide.net. Retrieved March 31, 2003 (http://www. wtg-online.com/data/yem/ yem580.asp).

INDEX

About the Author

Amy Romano is the author of five other titles for the Rosen Publishing Group. She has a master's degree in business administration from American International College in Springfield, Massachusetts, and has written a number of magazine articles on a range of topics for both consumer and business-to-business publications. Amy is a member of the adjunct faculty at Western International University in Arizona, where she lives with her husband, Don, and their children, Claudia, Sam, and Jack.

Acknowledgments

The author would like to extend a special thank-you to Jalal O. Yaqoub, economic and commercial attaché, and Fouad Al-Kohlani, assistant officer of economic affairs at the Embassy of the Republic of Yemen in Washington, D.C., for their considerable help. They were gracious and accommodating, and this book could not have been written without them.

Also, special thanks to Karin van der Tak for her expert guidance regarding matters pertaining to the Middle East and Asia.

Photo Credits

Cover (map), pp. 1 (foreground), 4–5, 48–49 © 2002 Geoatlas; cover (background), pp. 1 (background), 14, 15, 24, 25, 32–33, 44 courtesy of the General Libraries, the University of Texas at Austin; cover (top left), p. 53 © Thomas Hartwell/Time Life Pictures/Getty Images; cover (bottom left), p. 31 (inset) © Christine Osborne/Corbis; cover (bottom right) © Richard Bickel/Corbis; pp. 6, 11, 17, 20 © AKG Images/Jean-Louis Nou; p. 8 (top) © AKG Images/Gilles Mermet; pp. 8 (bottom), 10 (bottom) © David Forman/ Eye Ubiquitous/Corbis; p. 10 (top) © Archivo Iconografico, S.A./Corbis; p. 12 © Collart Herve/Corbis Sygma; pp. 18–19, 29, 30–31, 36–37, 52 maps designed by Tahara Hasan; pp. 22–23 © Historical Picture Archive/Corbis; p. 26 © Diego Lezama Orezzoli/Corbis; p. 27 © The Library of Congress, Geography and Map Division; p. 35 © Hulton-Deutsch Collection/Corbis; p. 38 © Bettmann/Corbis; pp. 39, 41 © Hulton/ Archive/Getty Images; pp. 45, 46, 50, 56, 57, 59 © AP/Wide World Photos; p. 51 © Robert Patrick/Corbis Sygma; p. 54 © AFP/Corbis; p. 55 © Maps.com/Corbis.

Designer: Tahara Hasan; **Editor:** Joann Jovinelly; **Photo Researcher:** Elizabeth Loving